K-Kids 1

John Kennedy

Word List

Core	
Stand up	Apple
Sit down	Bird
Come here	Cat
Turn around	Dog
Walk	Egg
Run	Fish
Jump	Gorilla
Skip	Heart
Go	Igloo
Stop	Jump rope
	Kangaroo
Take out your pencils	Lion
Put away your pencils	Moon
Open your books	Nest
Close your books	Octopus
	Peach
Make a line	Queen
Make a circle	Rabbit
Point to the board	Sun
Go to the board	Tiger
	Umbrella
	Violin
	Watch
	foX
	Yarn
	Zebra

Level 1	
Head	Circle
Shoulders	Rectangle
Knees	Heart
Toes	Diamond
Eyes	Triangle
Ears	Star
Mouth	
Nose	Dog
	Cat
Green	Bird
Orange	Cow
Purple	Rabbit
Black	Duck
Pink	
	Ride a bicycle
Sunny	Sing a song
Cloudy	Fly a kite
Windy	Bounce a ball
Rainy	Swim
Snowy	Smile
	Wink
Left	Dance
Right	
	1-10

Hello...

This is me...

Shapes

Numbers

3
5
8
10
6
7

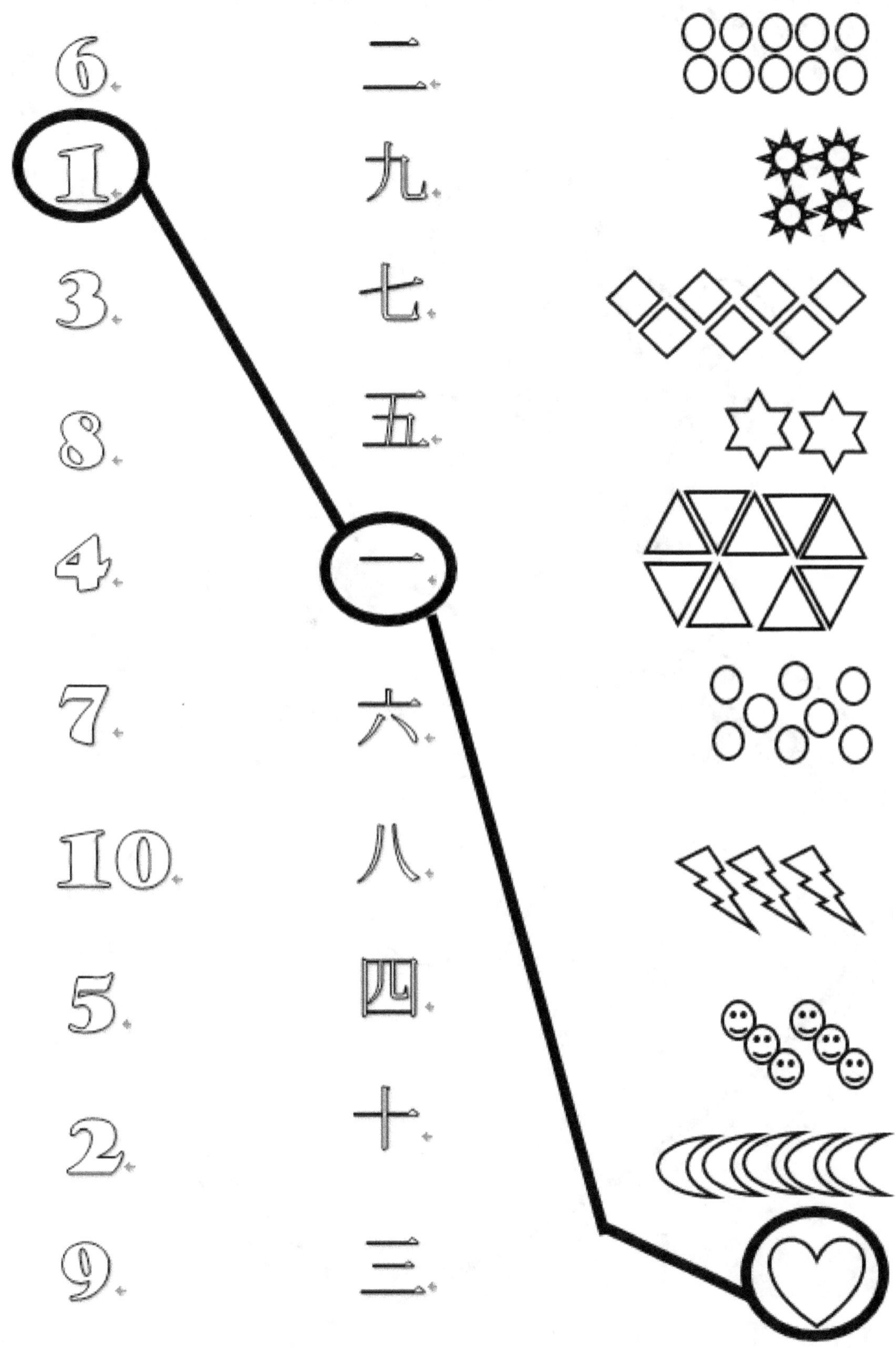

Happy Mothers Day

Colors

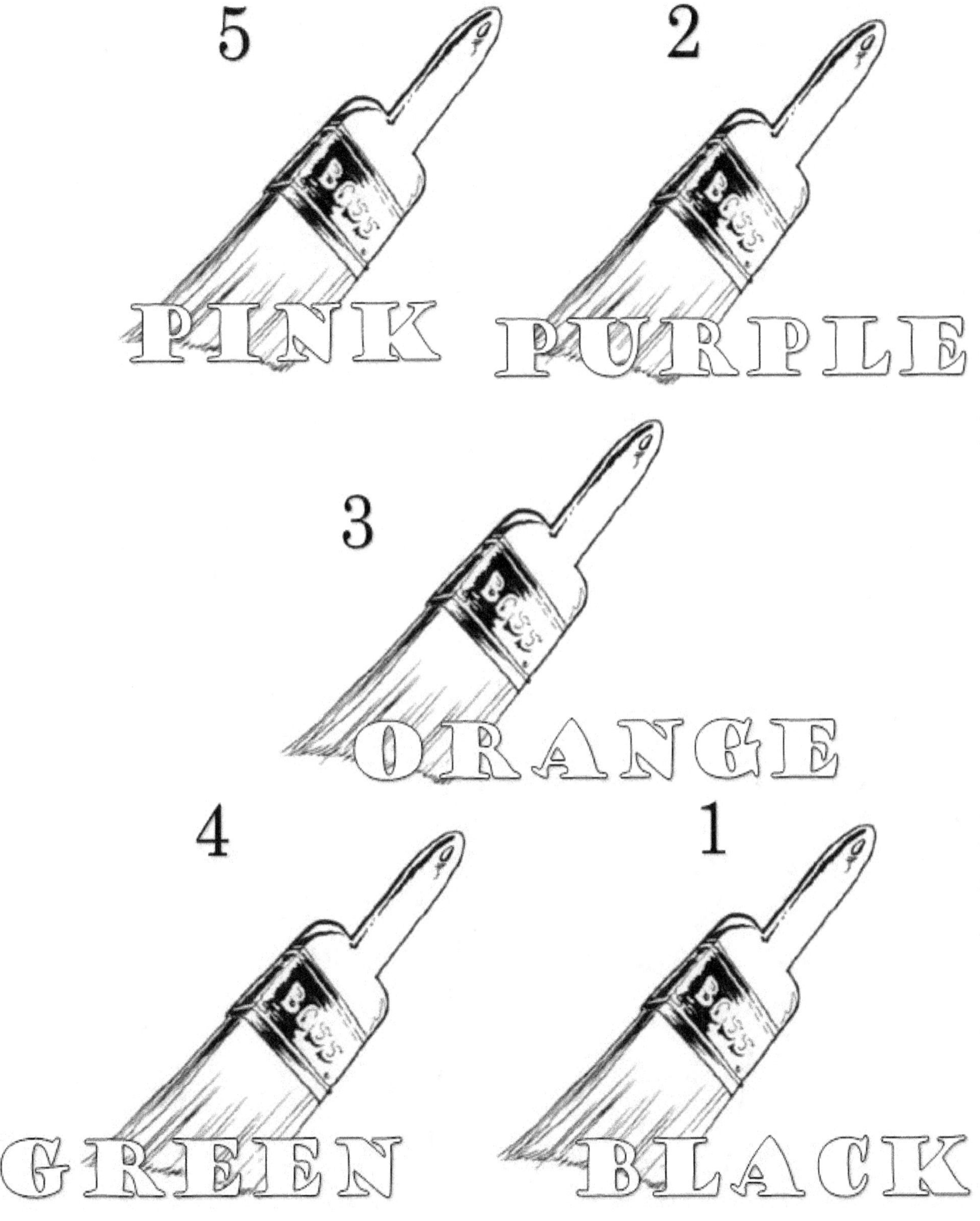

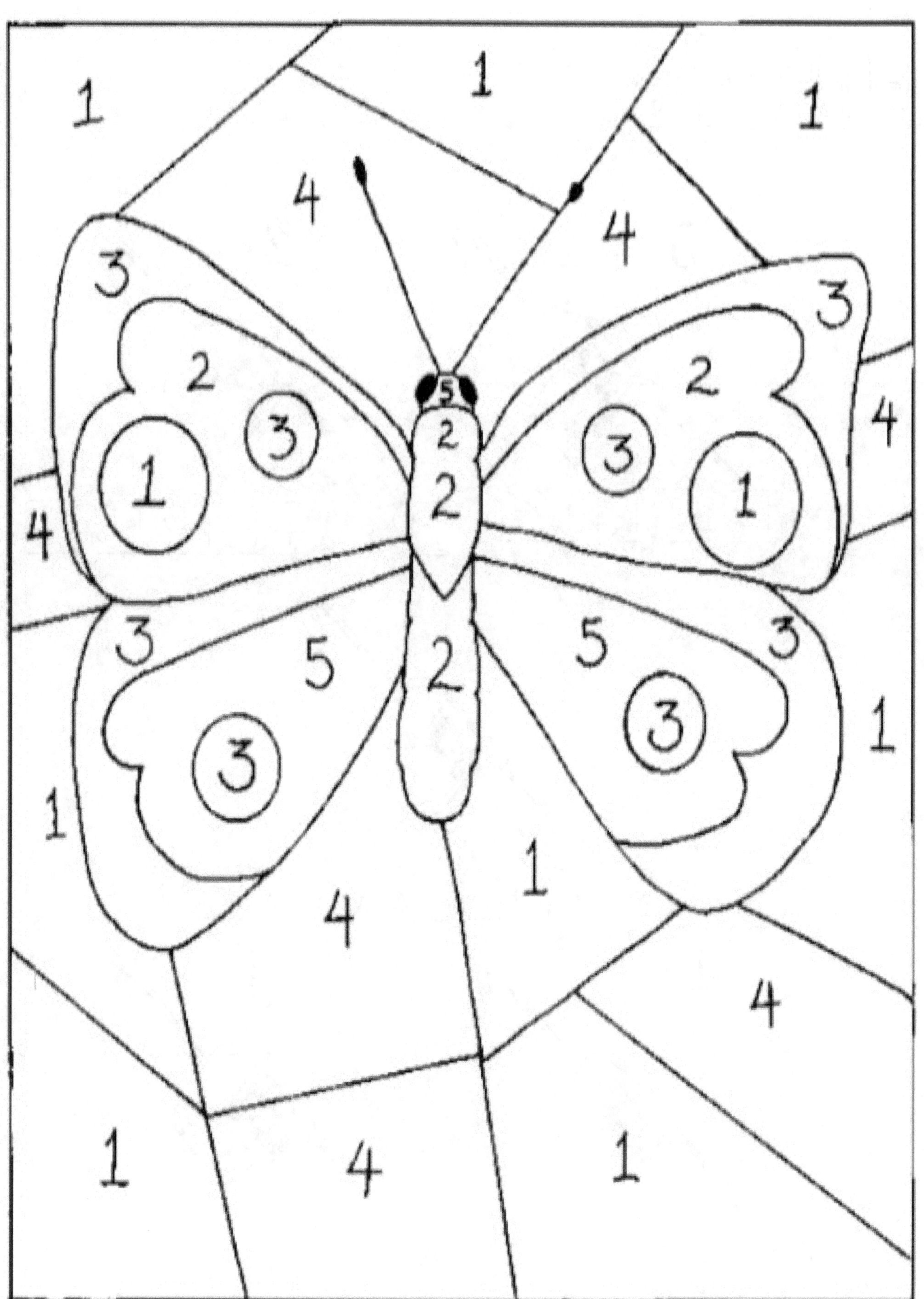

BINGO

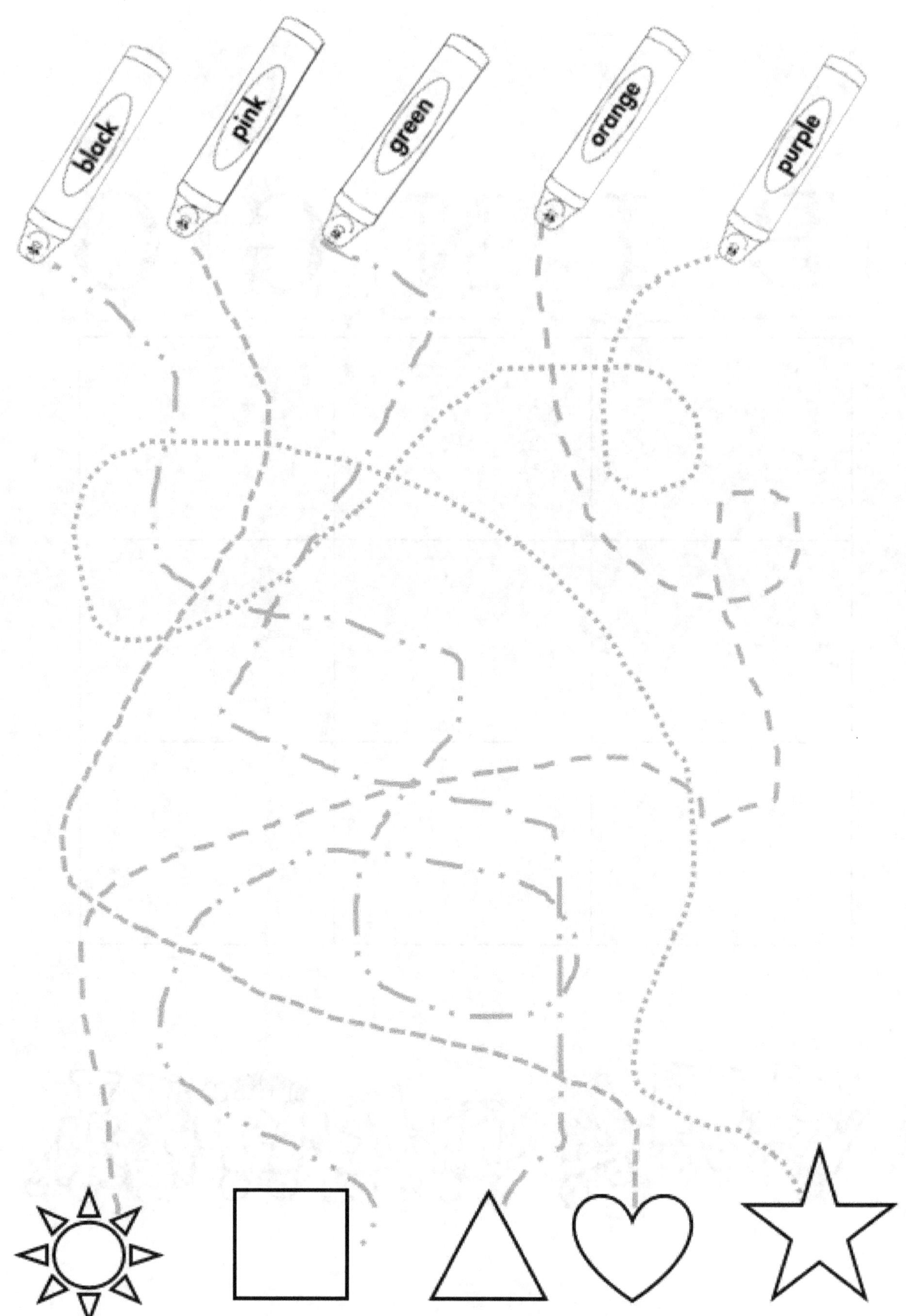

black
pink
green
orange
purple

ABC123

Spring Time

JULY
THE UNITED STATES
OF AMERICA

I'm hungry ...

Please.

I like eating ...

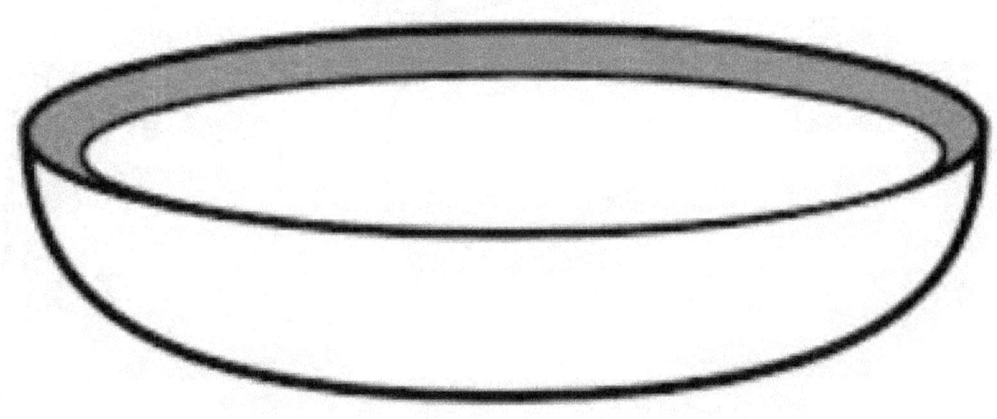

Whats that ?

It's a ....

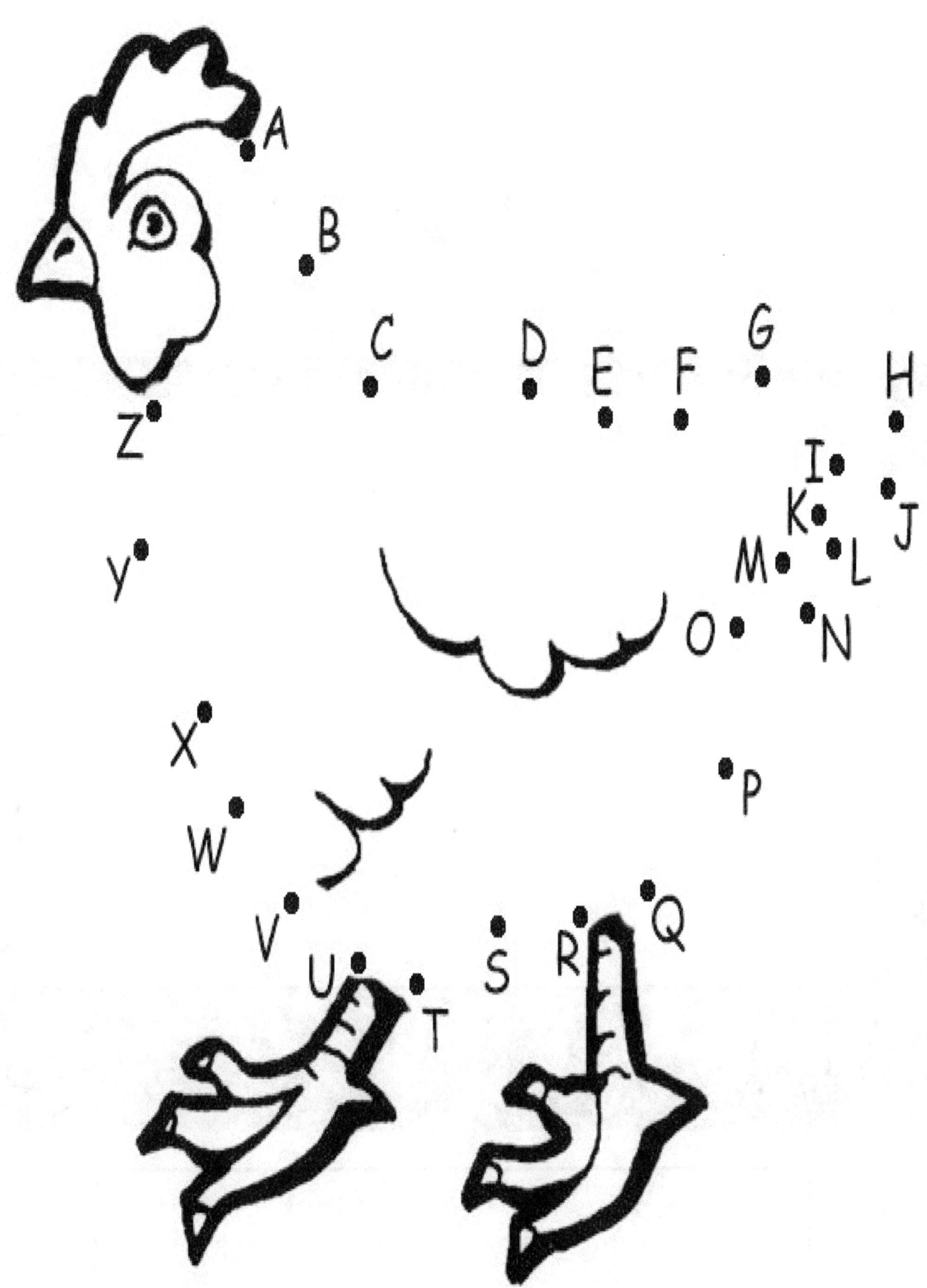

A
B
C
D
E
F
G
H
I
J
K
L
M
N
O
P
Q
R
S
T
U
V
W
X
Y
Z

I can ...

HAPPY HALLOWEEN

Body Parts

Body Parts

What to wear?

Hows the weather?

WEATHER

Left or Right?

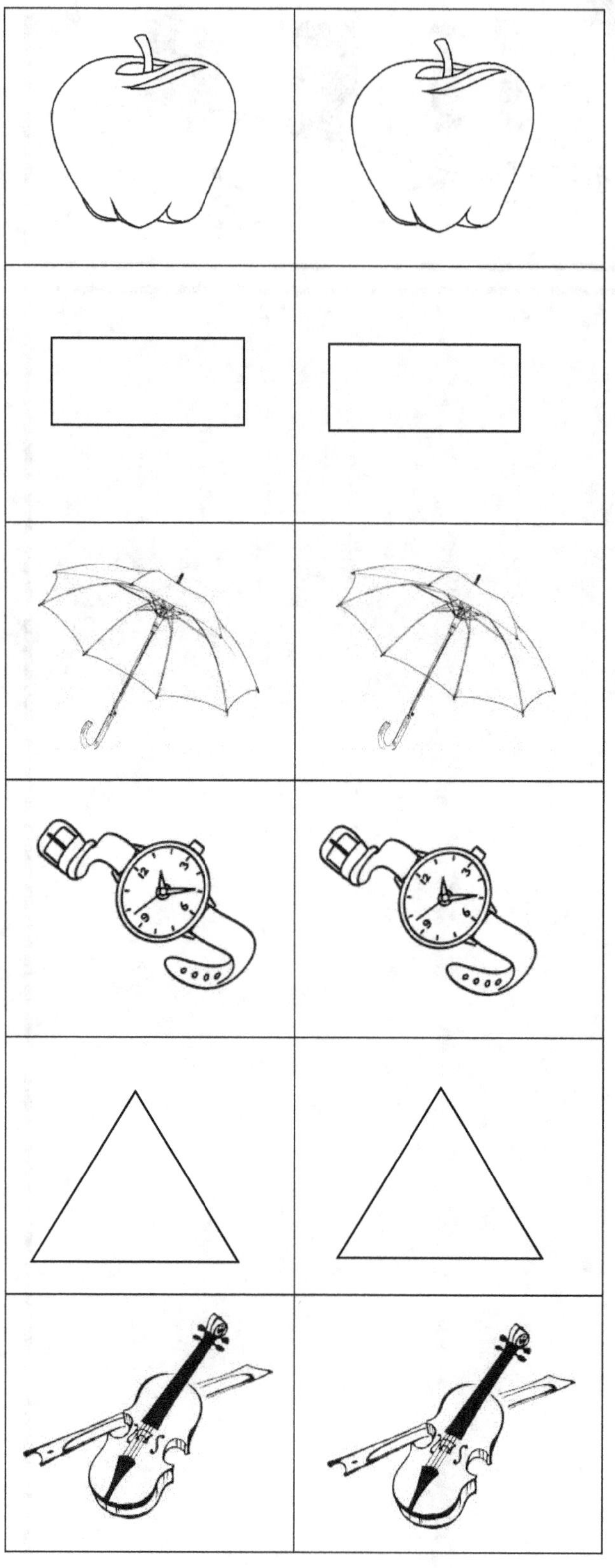

My Left Hand

ABC I know the XYZ
Alphabet!
Name
Date

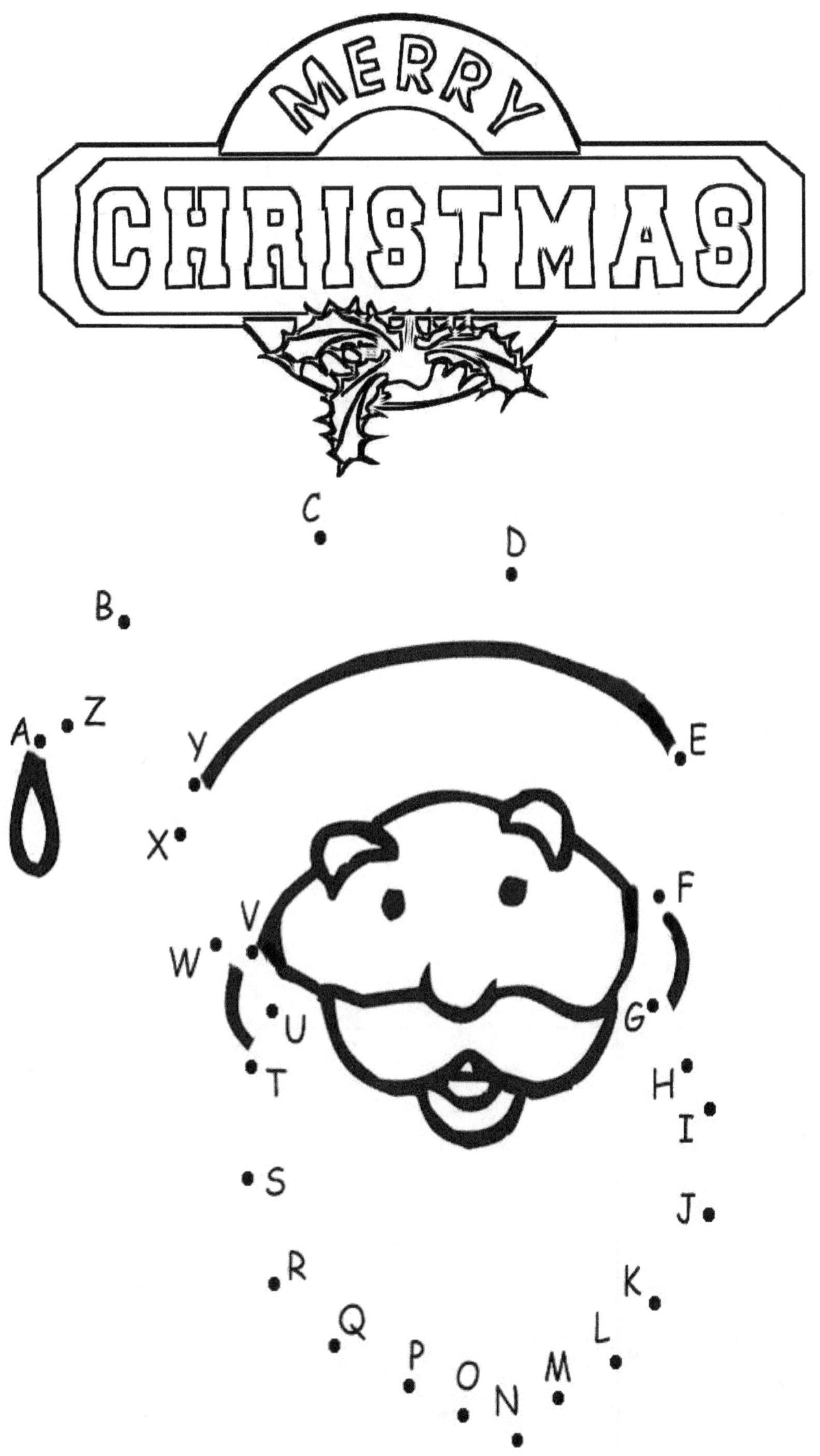

MERRY
CHRISTMAS

How many ...

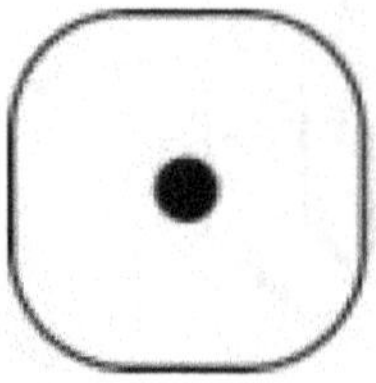

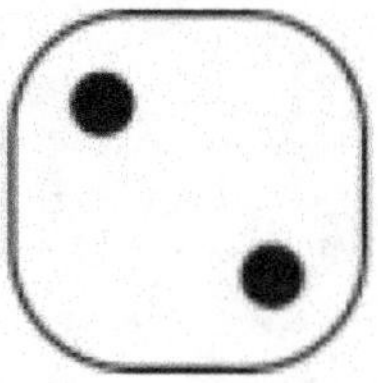

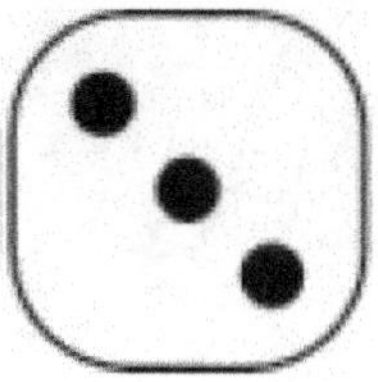

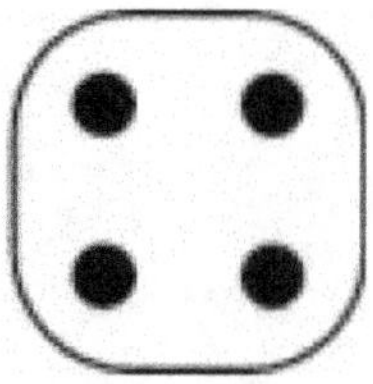

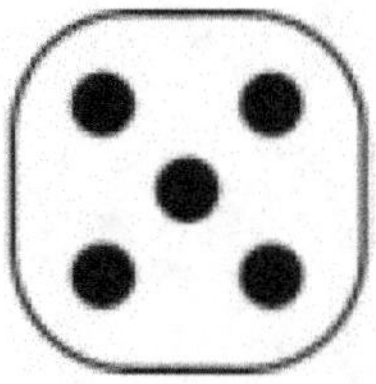

How many ...

How many times can you jump rope on ________________?

日 Sunday

月 Monday

火 Tuesday

水 Wednesday

木 Thursday

金 Friday

土 Saturday

What's next?

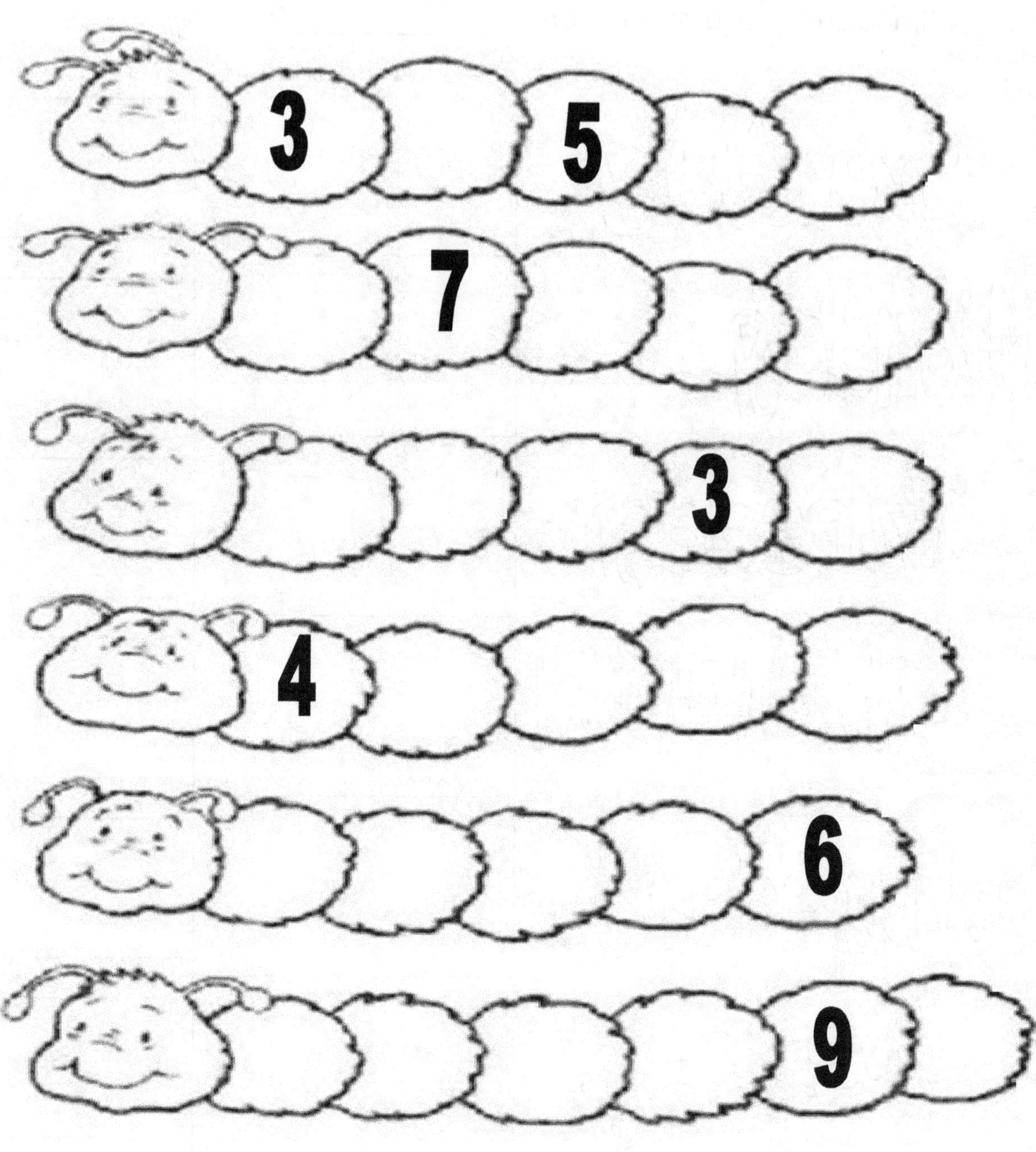

There are ...

	There are ____________ .... ____________ Lions
	There are ____________ .... ____________ Pigs
	There are ____________ .... ____________ Kangaroos
	There are ____________ .... ____________ Dogs
	There are ____________ .... ____________ Rabbits

It's a ...

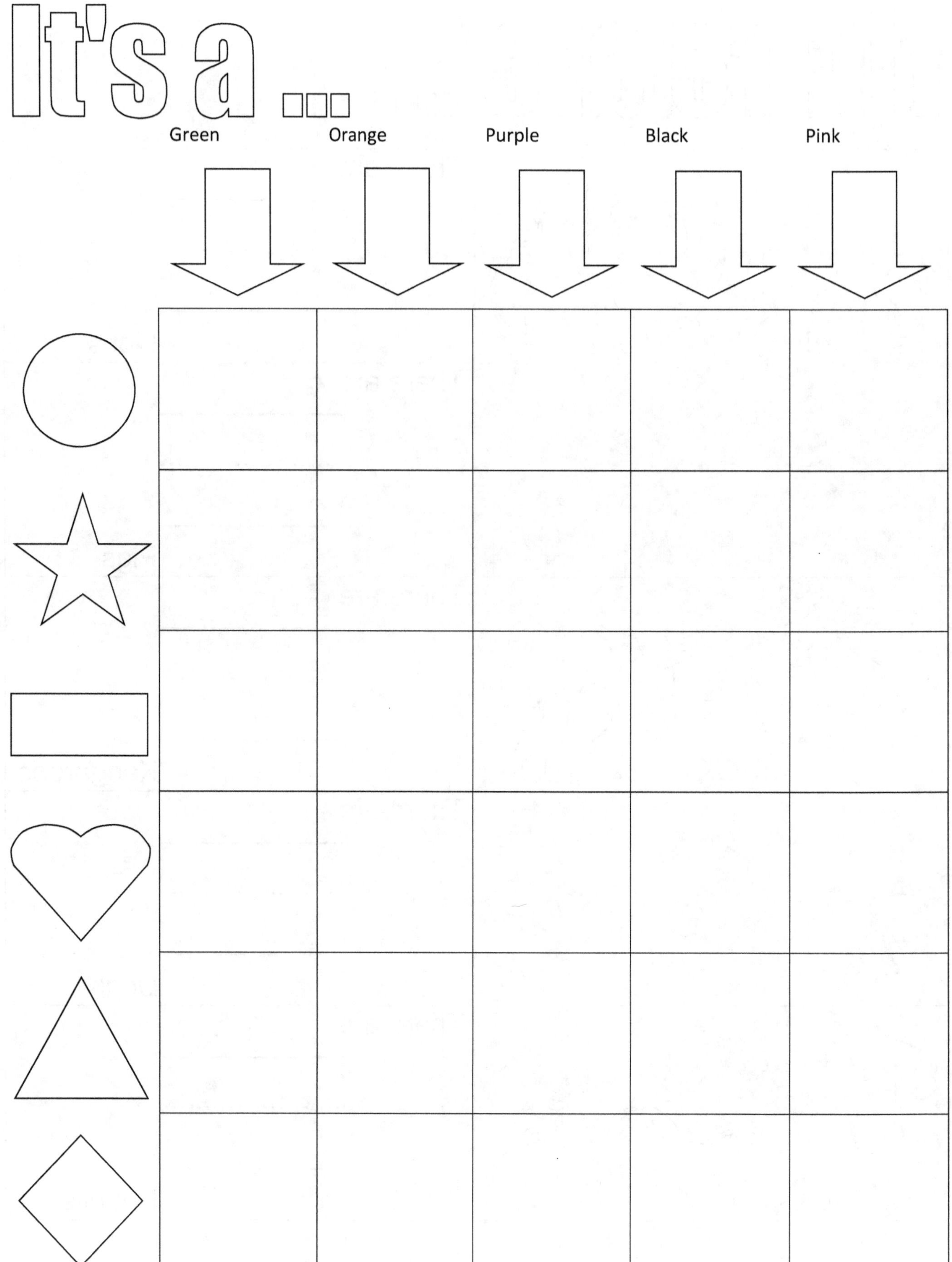

Tanigram adventure

Happy Valentine's Day

																			ONE
K	B	A	N	A															TWO
Y	O	Z	T	E	N	P	J												THREE
U	C	Y	K	P			X	I	P										FOUR
W	B	P	I	V	M				M	T	H								FIVE
Y	G	V	L	D	V	S				Y	F	P							SIX
E	N	C	Z	E	N	Y				N	X	I	F	I	V	E			SEVEN
T	W	O	O	R	G	S	S	I	J	P	S	E	V	E	N	Y	M	I G	EIGHT
K	A	R	Q	G	R	E	E	N	O	X	A	H	J	N	F	S	B	I M A	NINE
S	I	X	R	U	G	I	V	E	J	W	Q	E	T	Q	N	I	N	E O M U	TEN
M	B	L	A	C	K	E	X	O	G	A	Z	E	K	R	F	O	U	R N M W	GREEN
D	M	Q	R	O	Q	C	K	K	N	J	O	R	A	N	G	E	O	N E L G	ORANGE
U	M	A	C	P	U	R	P	L	E	I	G	H	T	C	F	X	U	M S R I	PURPLE
N	X	D	W	T	H	R	E	E	Z	T	J	P	W	Z	Z	O	O	W C	BLACK
	P	I	N	K								P	O	W	W				PINK
		P	W									T	K						

My Friends

Memories

Tanigram

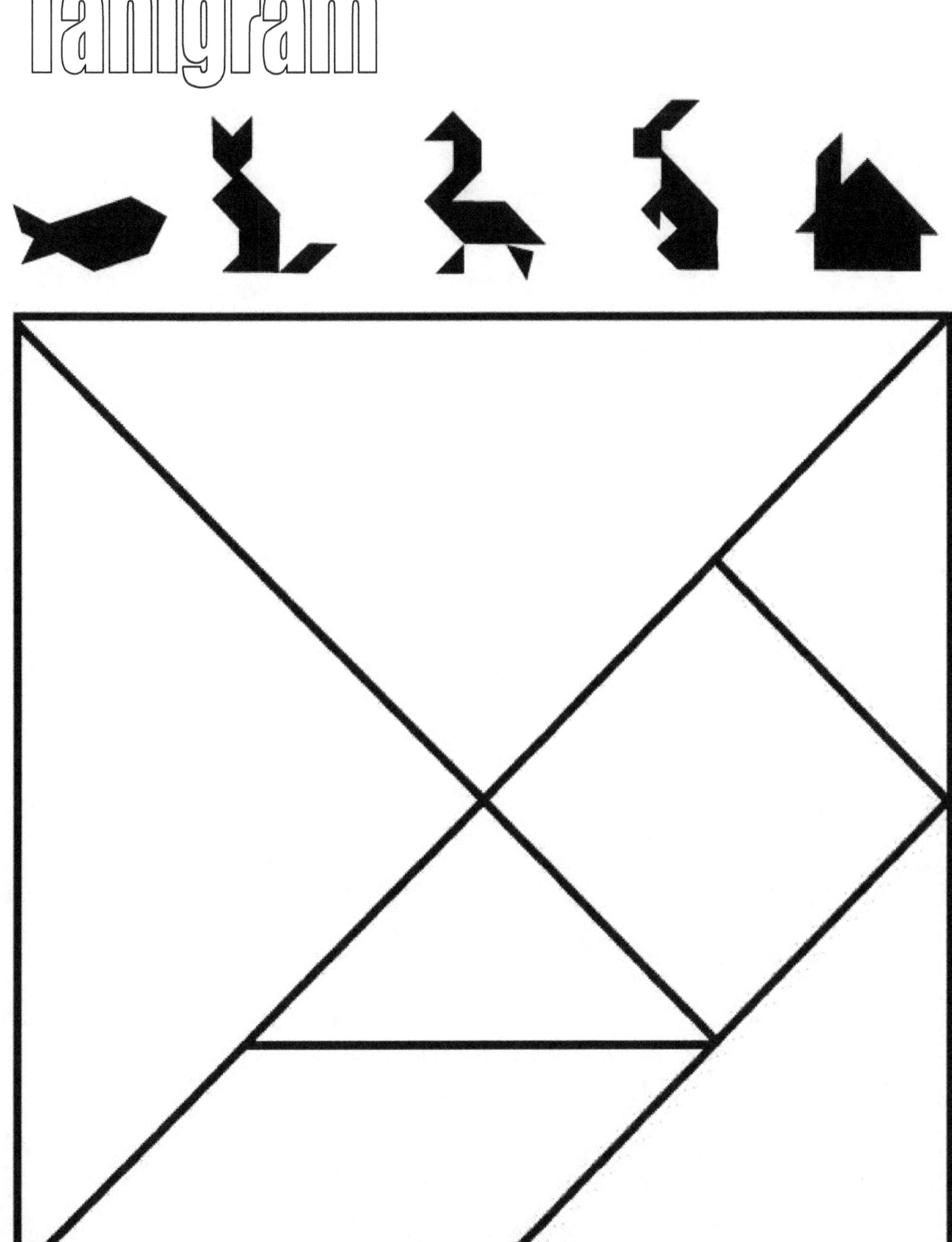

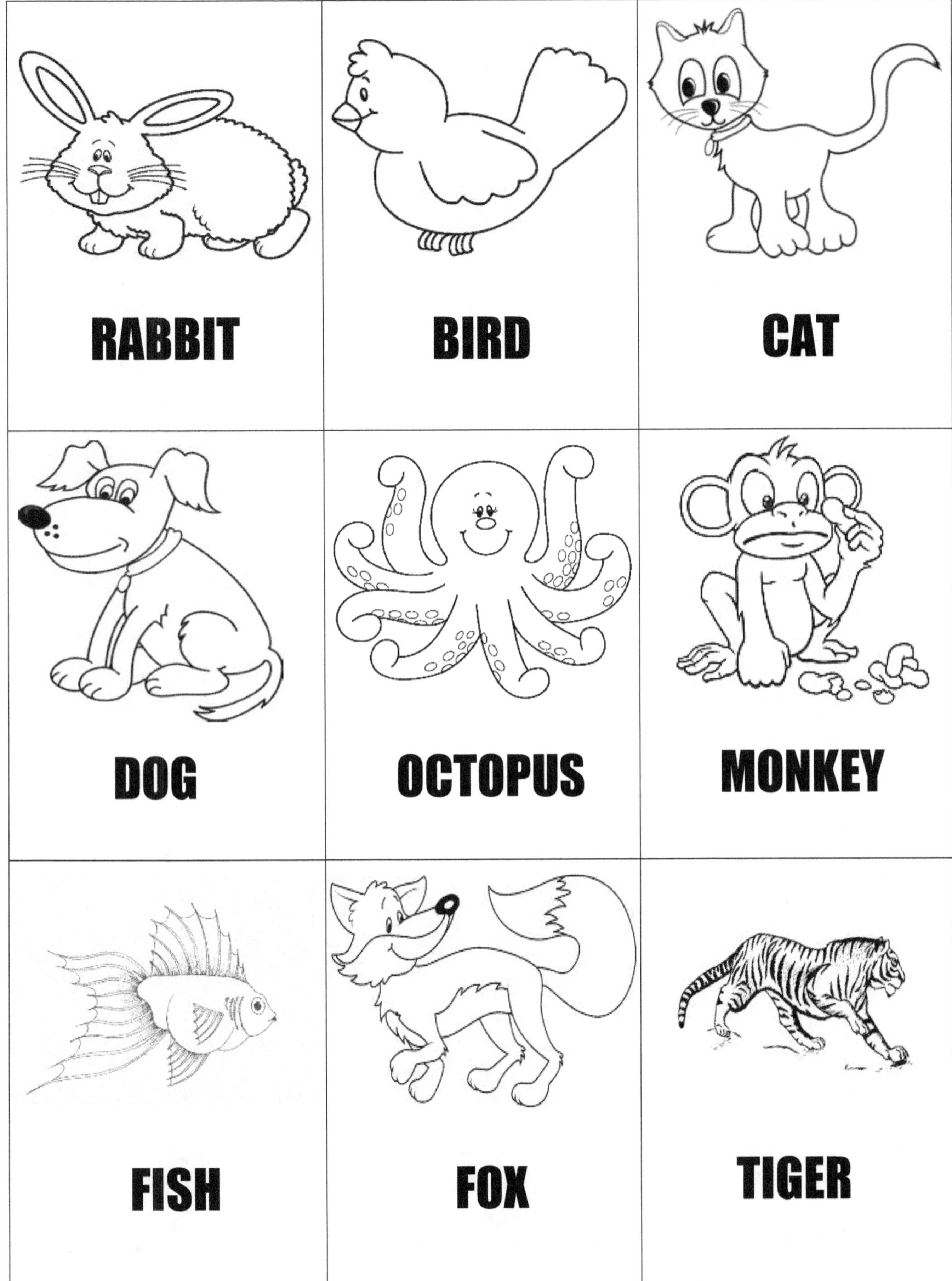

RABBIT
BIRD
CAT
DOG
OCTOPUS
MONKEY
FISH
FOX
TIGER

COW

ZEBRA

DUCK

GORILLA

KANGAROO

LION

CHICKEN

ELEPHANT

BEAR

MERRY CHRISTMAS

MERRY CHRISTMAS
MERRY CHRISTMAS

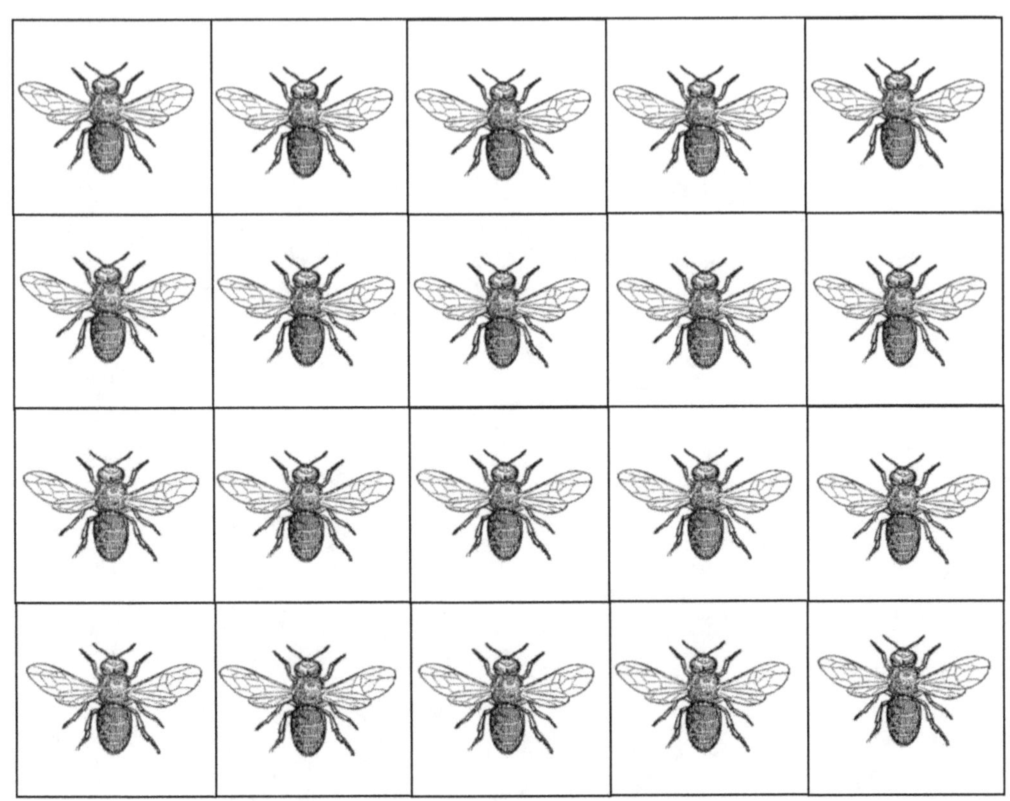

CERTIFICATE OF
COMPLETION
This is to certify that
Has successfully completed Book1

ACKNOLEDGEMENTS

A big thanks to the many teachers around the globe who's ideas and design have been a source for the materials in this book

To my wife for her support during the many time consuming projects that always seem to appear at the last minute.

To Mr. Yamanishi for the motivation to compile all this material together.

And finally to the students for who this was compiled for.